HIPPOPOTAMUSES

A TRUE BOOK

by
Melissa Stewart

Children's Press®
A Division of Scholastic Inc.

New York Toronto London Auckland Sydney
Mexico City New Delhi Hong Kong
Danbury, Connecticut

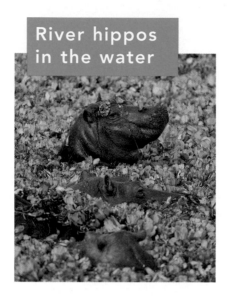

River hippos
in the water

Reading Consultant
Nanci R. Vargus, Ed.D.
Teacher in Residence
University of Indianapolis
Indianapolis, Indiana

Content Consultant
Kathy Carlstead, Ph.D.
Honolulu Zoo

Dedication:
To Colin Campbell Stewart

Library of Congress Cataloging-in-Publication Data

Stewart, Melissa
    Hippopotamuses / by Melissa Stewart.
        p. cm.—(A True book)
    Includes bibliographical references and index.
    ISBN 0-516-22200-7 (lib. bdg.)   0-516-26991-7 (pbk.)
    1. Hippopotamuses—Juvenile literature. [1. Hippopotamuses.] I. Title.
II. Series.
QL737.U57.S74 2002
599.63'5—dc21   2001017091

Contents

During the day, hippos stay in the water to keep cool.

A Hippo's Day

A river hippopotamus spends most of its day lounging and snoozing in a shallow water hole. Only its ears, eyes, and nose stick out of the water. The rest of its gigantic body stays underwater, where it is protected from the blazing hot African sun.

If you fell asleep in the water, you might drown. A hippo does not have to worry about that, though. When it takes a nap in the water, its body knows what to do. Every few minutes, the hippo automatically rises to the surface and takes a breath. Then the animal sinks again. The hippo does this without even thinking—the way you blink your eyes or sneeze.

When a hippo dives under-water, it holds its ears against

Hippos underwater

its head to keep the water out.
It also closes its nostrils tight.
A hippo can stay underwater
for about 5 minutes before it
needs a breath of fresh air.

Hippos sunning themselves

Sometimes a hippo comes onto shore to graze or warm up in the sun. When a hippo becomes too hot, it does not sweat the way you do. To stay cool, it may wallow in mud. A

A hippo rolling in the mud

thick layer of mud also keeps biting insects away from the hippo's skin.

When a hippo really heats up, a pink oil oozes out of its skin. This oil keeps the animal's skin moist. It also acts

Pink oil oozing
from the skin of
a hippo

as sunscreen. The oil may even
help keep cuts and wounds
clean so that they do not get
infected.

At night, a hippo lumbers
out of the water. It follows a

well-worn trail that leads to its nighttime grazing grounds. Hippos mark these trails with dung. Sometimes these dung heaps can become quite large!

Most hippos travel 3 to 6 miles (5 to 10 kilometers) in search of food. For most of the night, a hippo munches noisily on grass and leaves. Sometimes it lies down and takes a short nap.

A hippo grabs each mouth-ful of grass or leaves with its

Hippos search for food mainly at night.

lips. Then the animal swings its head from side to side until it tears the plant free. The hippo uses its giant tongue to move the food to the back of its mouth. It

grinds the food with its teeth and then swallows.

Just before sunrise, the hippo traces its trail back to the water. It finds its way by following the scent of its own dung.

All About Hippos

The river hippo is one of the largest animals on land. A hippo may be up to 4.6 feet (1.4 meters) tall at the shoulder and 16.6 feet (5.1 m) long. Most hippos weigh about 3,300 pounds (1,500 kilograms), but some weigh more than 9,000 pounds

The river hippo is one of the world's largest land animals.

(4,080 kg). That's more than the weight of three cars!

Hippos have lived on Earth for more than 25 million years. Until about 10,000 years ago,

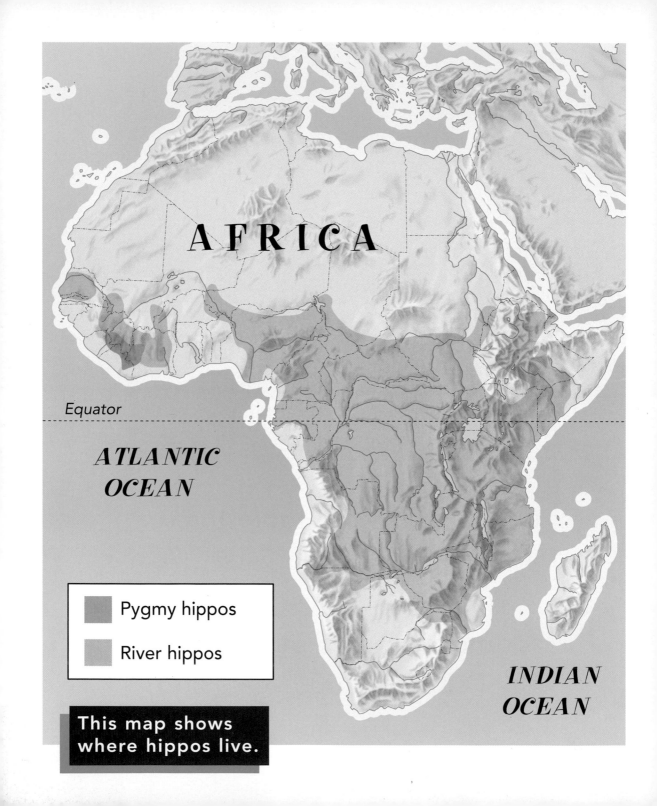

AFRICA

Equator

ATLANTIC
OCEAN

INDIAN
OCEAN

Pygmy hippos

River hippos

This map shows
where hippos live.

they were common through-
out Asia, Africa, and Central
Europe. Today they are found
only in a few parts of Africa.

The name *hippopotamus*
comes from two Greek words
that mean "river horse." A
hippo does not have much in
common with a horse, though.
It is more closely related to
pigs, camels, and giraffes. All
of these animals eat mainly
plants and have an even number of toes on each foot.

Like camels (above) and giraffes (right), hippos (below) have an even number of toes.

Camels and giraffes have two toes on each foot. A hippo has four toes on each foot. The stretchy skin between a hippo's toes helps it swim. When a hippo steps onto land, its toes spread out wide so that the huge animal can support all its weight. Pads on the bottom of each foot soften the impact of the hippo's heavy footsteps.

A hippo and a horse do have some things in common.

They both belong to a group of animals called mammals. All mammals have a backbone that supports their body and helps them move. They also have lungs and breathe air.

Mammals are warm-blooded animals, so their body temperature stays about the same no matter how cold or warm their surroundings are. Baby mammals grow inside their mother's body until they are ready to be born. Then they feed on

A female hippo protects and cares for her newborn calf.

mother's milk until they are able to eat solid food.

All mammals have one more thing in common—hair. You

might think a hippo has no hair, but it does have a little hair around its ears and at the end of its tail. A hippo also has whiskers and eyelashes.

A Hippo's Body

A river hippo's large head, barrel-shaped body, and short heavy legs make it easy to recognize. The thick, wrinkly skin on a hippo's back protects the hippo from enemies.

Most animals have eyes on the sides of their head. A hippo's eyes are on top of its

The river hippo has a large head and short, thick legs.

head—as are its ears and nostrils. A hippo can keep most of its head underwater and still see, hear, and breathe.

When a hippo is in the water, its back is a good place for hungry birds to perch.

When you grow up, you will have about thirty-two teeth in your mouth. An adult hippo has about forty-two teeth. It

has four long, curved teeth in front. On each side of these are two tusklike canine teeth. The hippo uses these teeth during fights with other hippos. It uses its back teeth to eat.

Pygmy Hippos

The river hippo has a smaller cousin called the pygmy hippo. The pygmy hippo is very rare and shy. It lives deep in the rain forests and swamps of West Africa and eats leaves, stems, roots, and fallen fruits.

The pygmy hippo is about the same size as a large hog. It has a dark back and a grayish-yellow or cream belly. It spends more time on land than the river hippo. That is why its body looks different.

The pygmy hippo's head is rounder, and its eyes are on the side of its head. This allows the hippo to see ahead and to the sides as it wanders through the forest. Also, its legs are longer and thinner than those of the river hippo, and its feet are smaller. Its toes have sharp nails, and there is no skin between them.

Hippo Battles

Most river hippos live in herds of ten to fifteen animals. Some hippo herds have as many as 100 members. Male hippos, or bulls, mark their territories with dung. As a bull produces dung, it rapidly flips its tail back and forth. This scatters

A large herd of hippos

the droppings—and the bull's scent—for several yards.

Most of the time, hippos are peaceful animals. But when one male enters the territory of another male, there may be trouble. When a bull spots an

Hippos threatening each other

intruder, he opens his mouth as wide as he can and shows his long, sharp teeth. The intruder usually retreats, and peace is restored. Sometimes, though, the intruder opens his mouth wide—returning the threat.

Then the hippos growl, honk, roar, snort, and charge with their mouths open. If they are in the water, they may toss water at or bite each other.

A hippo biting another hippo

Many male hippos have scars from battle wounds.

If they are on land, each bull slashes at the other's front legs. The fight may last for hours, and sometimes one hippo is killed. If you look at the skin of an adult male hippo, you will probably see scars from his battle wounds.

A Hippo's Life

When it is time for a female hippo to give birth, she leaves the herd and goes to a quiet place. A baby hippo is usually born underwater. It must rise to the surface to take its first breath. A hippo calf can walk a few hours after it is born, and quickly learns to swim and run.

A baby hippo can walk soon after it is born.

A newborn hippo weighs from 55 to 120 pounds (25 to 54 kg). Feeding on mother's milk, the calf gains about 10 pounds (4.5 kg) a day. After about 4 months, the young hippo begins to eat plants.

Around the time it is 8 months old, the hippo stops nursing.

When the calf is a few weeks old, its mother returns to the herd and the baby joins other calves in a nursery. The young hippos enjoy playing with one

A hippo calf begins to eat plants when it is about 4 months old.

Young hippos playfighting

another. They have mock battles, roll around in the water, and play hide-and-seek.

One or two females watch all the young in the nursery so that the mothers can rest and feed. The babysitters protect the calves from lions, hyenas, and crocodiles. They also watch for male hippos that might accidentally step on a little calf.

Outside the nursery, a calf stays close to its mother. It may climb onto her back for a rest—or just because it's fun to jump off.

A hippo calf stays close to its mother.

A female usually gives birth to only one baby at a time, but up to four calves may live with her. When the hippo family grazes, the young form a single-file line behind their mother. The youngest calf is always closest to its mother. If one of the calves misbehaves, the mother bumps it with her huge head.

Hippos are ready to have young of their own when they are a few years old, but many don't mate until they are older.

A mother hippo with calves of different ages

Hippos usually mate in the water—with a lot of noise and splashing—at the end of the dry season. When the baby is born 8 months later, it is in the middle of the wet season. There is plenty of food.

In Danger— and Dangerous

Like other large African animals, hippos are now in danger. Only about 157,000 river hippos and just 2,000 pygmy hippos are alive today. In the past, people killed river hippos for their tusk-like teeth and their skins. Pygmy hippos were killed for food. Today, most hippos live in

Lake Manyara National Park in Tanzania is among the places where hippos are protected.

national parks, where they are protected from hunters.

Hippos seem big and bulky, but they are strong and can move fast. This makes them a threat to humans. If a person gets between a hippo and the

When a hippo becomes angry, it may charge.

water or between a mother and a calf, the animal will attack. A hippo can outrun a person on land and outswim a person in the water. A person has little chance of escaping from an angry hippo. Hippos kill about 300 people every year.

Like all animals, hippos are an important part of our world. We must work to save them, but we must also be careful of them. They can be fierce animals, so it is best to watch and enjoy them from a distance.

It is safest to enjoy hippos from a distance.

To Find Out More

Here are some additional resources to help you learn more about hippopotamuses:

 **Books**

Denis-Huot, Christine. **The Hippopotamus.** Charlesbridge, 1994.

Lewen, Betsy. **Chubbo's Pool.** Clarion, 1996.

Patent, Dorothy Hinshaw. **Why Mammals Have Fur.** Cobble Hill Books, 1995.

Stewart, Melissa. **Mammals.** Children's Press, 2001.

Walker, Sally M. **Hippos.** Carolrhoda, 1997.

☼ Organizations and Online Sites

Hippopotamus
http://home.vicnet.net.au/ ~neils/africa/hippo.htm

This site features information about hippos and pictures of them in their natural environment.

Hippopotamus
http://www.birmingham-zoo.com/ao/mammal/ hippo.htm

Check out a variety of photos and movies of the hippopotamuses at Birmingham Zoo in Alabama. This site also includes some basic facts about hippos.

Hippopotamus
http://www.whozoo.org/ Intro98/herrick/sethherr .htm

This site has answers to all your questions about hippos. It even includes information about research on hippos.

International Wildlife Coalition
70 East Falmouth Highway
East Falmouth, MA, USA
02536
http://www.iwc.org

The IWC works to save endangered species and preserve animal habitats and the environment.

Pygmy Hippopotamus
http://www.ultimateungu-late.com/pygmyhippo.html

Pygmy hippos may be rare, but this site has a lot of information about them. It also includes a few photos.

KidsGoWild
http://wcs.org/sites/ kidsgowild

This is the kids' page of the Wildlife Conservation Society. It includes wildlife news, wild animal facts, and information on how kids can get involved in saving wild animals and the environment by joining Conservation Kids.

45

Important Words

bull name for the male of some kinds of mammals, including hippos

calf name for the young of some kinds of mammals, including hippos

canine teeth pointed teeth near the front of a hippo's mouth

dung animal droppings

intruder unwelcome visitor

mammal warm-blooded animal that has a backbone and hair and feeds its young with mother's milk

mock not real; done as part of play

nursery area where young hippos stay so that females can protect them from danger

territory area where an animal lives, hunts, mates, and raises young

warm-blooded maintaining a body temperature that stays about the same whatever the surroundings

Index

Meet the Author

A few years ago, Melissa Stewart visited the African countries of Kenya and Tanzania. While on safari, she was captivated by hippos. She saw dozens of them hanging out in waterholes to avoid the hot, mid-afternoon sun.

Ms. Stewart earned a bachelor's degree in biology from Union College and a master's degree in science and environmental journalism from New York University. She has written more than twenty books for children. Ms. Stewart lives in Marlborough, Massachusetts.